Out and About Activity Book

Nature

By
Gillian Osband
Illustrations by
Dave Simonds

Contents

Kingfisher

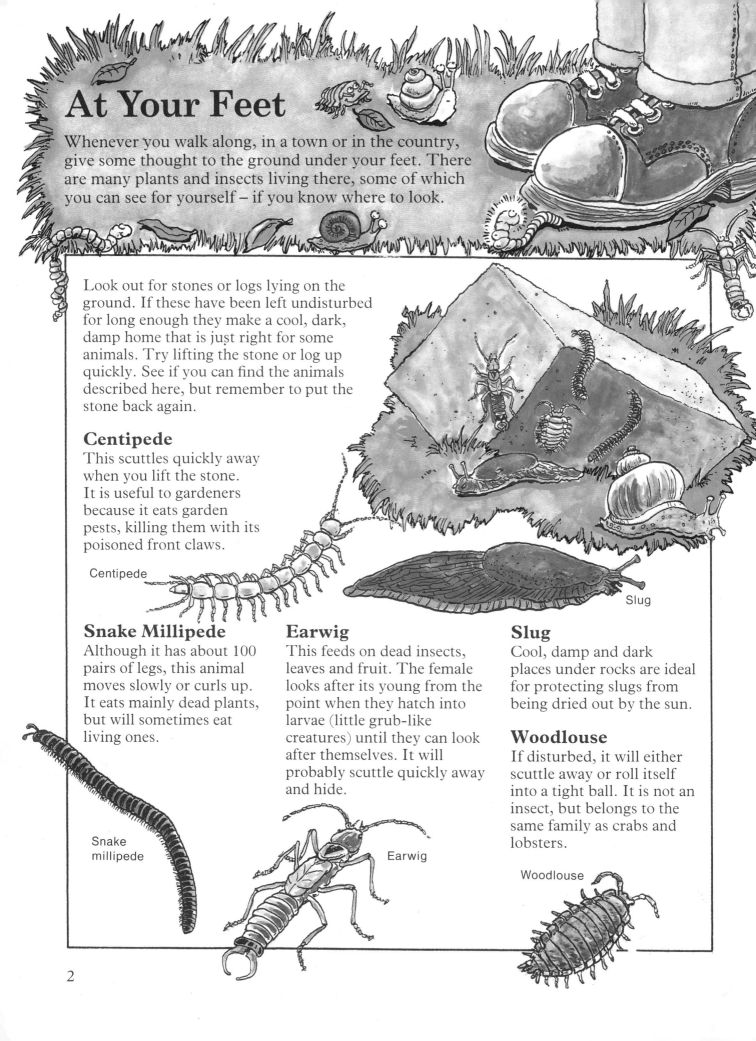

At Your Feet

Whenever you walk along, in a town or in the country, give some thought to the ground under your feet. There are many plants and insects living there, some of which you can see for yourself – if you know where to look.

Look out for stones or logs lying on the ground. If these have been left undisturbed for long enough they make a cool, dark, damp home that is just right for some animals. Try lifting the stone or log up quickly. See if you can find the animals described here, but remember to put the stone back again.

Centipede

This scuttles quickly away when you lift the stone. It is useful to gardeners because it eats garden pests, killing them with its poisoned front claws.

Centipede

Slug

Snake Millipede

Although it has about 100 pairs of legs, this animal moves slowly or curls up. It eats mainly dead plants, but will sometimes eat living ones.

Snake millipede

Earwig

This feeds on dead insects, leaves and fruit. The female looks after its young from the point when they hatch into larvae (little grub-like creatures) until they can look after themselves. It will probably scuttle quickly away and hide.

Earwig

Slug

Cool, damp and dark places under rocks are ideal for protecting slugs from being dried out by the sun.

Woodlouse

If disturbed, it will either scuttle away or roll itself into a tight ball. It is not an insect, but belongs to the same family as crabs and lobsters.

Woodlouse

Keeping Woodlice

You need: a clear plastic box and a lid with air holes.

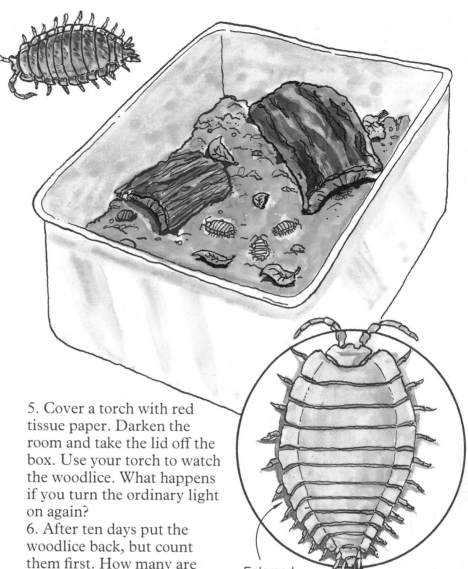

1. Put moist soil in the box to a depth of 6cm. Place some dead leaves, stones or pebbles and, if possible, tree bark on top.

2. Look under a stone or brick for some woodlice. Scoop some up quickly but gently, using a spoon, and put them into the box. Try to collect about 20. Count them as you put them in.

3. Take one out to study, but don't let the others escape. The body is made up of 13 segments. Try and count them all, and look at its head too. Gently turn it on its back. Can you see its feelers, and count its legs? Now put it back in the box.

4. Keep the soil damp and give your woodlice fresh food every day. They enjoy fresh cabbage or lettuce or a bit of carrot.

5. Cover a torch with red tissue paper. Darken the room and take the lid off the box. Use your torch to watch the woodlice. What happens if you turn the ordinary light on again?

6. After ten days put the woodlice back, but count them first. How many are there now?

Enlarged woodlouse

Make a 'Hidden World' Map

You can make a map of a park or garden you have explored, showing all the places where you spotted 'hidden' animals.

Draw a map of the place, showing trees, paths and other details. Then draw in the animals you found, in the correct places.

On another piece of paper, draw the stones or logs under which the animals were hiding, with a flap on each one, as shown.

Cut them out and fold the flaps right back.

Glue the flaps onto the map to hide the animals. You can lift the stones and logs up to find the animals, just as you did outside.

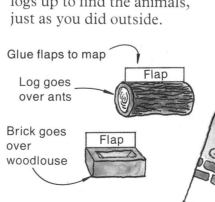

Glue flaps to map →

Log goes over ants

Brick goes over woodlouse

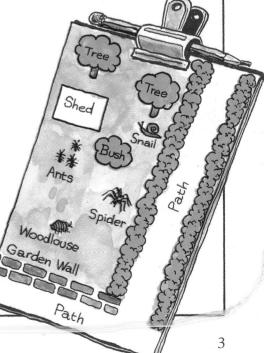

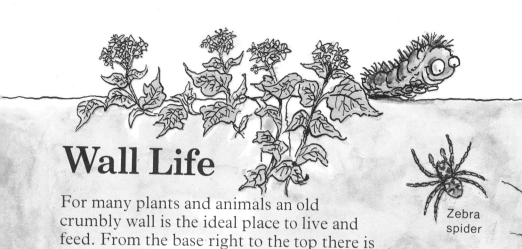

Wall Life

For many plants and animals an old crumbly wall is the ideal place to live and feed. From the base right to the top there is always plenty going on – and plenty for you to see and discover.

Zebra spider

Spiders

There are nearly 600 different types of spider in Britain. In a medium-sized garden there could be up to one million spiders. They are carnivores (they eat animals, not plants), and feed on small insects which they catch in their webs.

Diadem spiders spin most of the large webs you will see. If you find a web, study it carefully but don't touch it – they are easily damaged. Can you see a spider in its lair nearby? This may be a crack in a wall or a silk tube it spins for itself. Try and draw a web pattern.

Diadem spider

Maidenhair fern

Lichen

Snails and Slugs

Their scientific name is *gastropods*, which means 'stomach-foot'. They have one large foot along the base of their body, and their stomach is inside it. Remains of gastropods have been found in fossils millions of years old, so we know they have been around for a long time. Their bodies are soft, but although snails have shells to protect them from drying up or being eaten by birds, slugs have to hide in cool damp places under stones, and only come out at night to feed.

Ferns, Mosses and Lichens

These all belong to a family of plants called *cryptograms*, which first appeared on Earth 350 million years ago. Fossils of the remains of these plants show that some of them have hardly changed in all that time.

Lichens

If you find lichen on a wall, try looking at it through a magnifying glass. It will look strange – like grey, crusty leaves or a yellow stain. In fact, it is made up of two types of plant, a type of algae and a fungus, growing together. Each helps the other to survive.

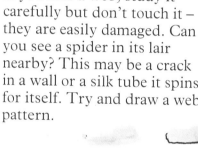

Snail

Toad

Slug

Make a Flowering Wall

If you have a wall in your garden, ask permission before you start planting. Or build a small one of mud and stones.

Some wild flowers, such as stonecrop and ivy-leaved toadflax will grow in cracks in walls, and you can add garden plants too. Honeysuckle climbs to cover a large area, and its scented flowers attract many insects. So do virginian stocks and the poached egg flower.

Try hanging an old kettle on the wall, fairly high up. A robin may use it to nest in.

Ivy-leaved toadflax

Stonecrop in crevices

Honeysuckle to climb

Kettle for robin to nest in

Wasp

Bee

Birds and Beasts

Some birds build their nests in climbing plants, or visit them to feed, pecking up insects and seeds.

Small animals, such as voles, field mice and toads may make their homes in the sheltered area at the base of an old wall.

Field mouse

Bees and Wasps

Most types are solitary, and live on their own. Many visit gardens and nest in holes in walls. Some bees are so small they nest in holes only 1cm across.

Bottom to Top

Look at any old walls near your home where plants grow undisturbed. The conditions are different all the way up. At the base, there is more shelter and moisture. Farther up, there may be deep cracks for plants to take root. On top, the wall is exposed to the wind and sun, and plants have to be tough to survive.

King of the Soil

Did you know that if you have a medium-sized garden with good soil there could be as many as a quarter of a million earthworms living there? There are about 25 different types of earthworm in this country. Some are red or pink, others are yellowish or grey-brown. Carefully dig some up and see how many different types you can find. All of them play an important part in keeping your garden healthy.

Body may have 75–250 ringed segments

Pointed head

The clitellum – a lighter band or ring nearer its head than its tail

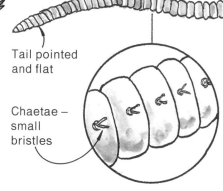

Tail pointed and flat

Chaetae – small bristles

How Worms Move

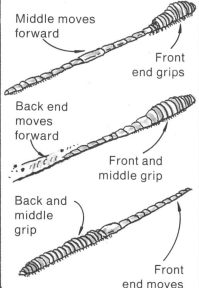

Front end moves forward and gets thinner

Bristles grip earth at middle and back

Each segment is lifted from the ground in turn

Middle moves forward

Front end grips

Back end moves forward

Front and middle grip

Back and middle grip

Front end moves forward

Great Gardeners

If there are flints or stones on the surface of your garden, in 30 years they will have been buried under 17.5cm of soil brought to the surface by earthworms.

Earthworms are great cultivators. They bore and burrow in the soil, loosening it to let in air and water, which the plant roots need to keep them healthy. Earthworms also act as manure spreaders – they eat tiny pieces of dead plants mixed with soil. The waste soil passes through their bodies and is left behind as small lumps of fine, fertile soil known as 'worm casts'.

Earthworms can do all this, and they are only 10–30cm in length.

Worm Facts

Every year worms may recycle ten tonnes of new soil over every acre of land.

In a drought, an earthworm will burrow down 24–30 metres to find moisture, lining its burrows with a sticky fluid as it goes to stop the walls collapsing.

Earthworms do have a small brain but they seem to manage quite well without it. They do sometimes grow a new one, however, so it must be used for something.

Earthworms are *herm-aphrodites* – both male and female at the same time. Any two adult earthworms can form a mating pair, and both lay fertile eggs.

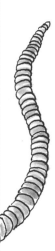

A Wormery

1. Find a large jam jar with a lid. Make some holes in the lid to let air in.

2. Place damp garden soil in the jar, to a depth of about 4cm. Cover it with a layer of sand about 2cm deep. Add more layers until the jar is about three-quarters full.

3. Stick a strip of paper on the outside and mark the position of the layers.

4. Carefully dig up about six earthworms and put them in the jar.

5. Find out what they like to eat by laying different things on top of the soil. Try cheese, lettuce and different leaves.

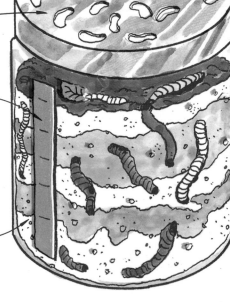

Air holes in lid

Strip of paper to mark layers

Layers of soil and sand

6. Watch what happens over the next few days. What happens to the layers? Can you see any worm casts? What food have they chosen?

7. Once you have seen the worms at work, put them back in the garden, preferably in the evening, when it is cooler.

Worms of Art

You need: poster paints, water, saucers or tin foil containers, paper, a rag and old newspapers (for the mess), your hand.

First spread newspaper on the surface where you are working. Put a different colour paint in each saucer, but keep a couple empty for mixing colours too.

Experiment with dipping your fingers and finger-tips in the paint and onto the paper. This can be messy, so keep the rag close by to wipe your hands on.

Adjust the thickness of the paint until you like the effect you are getting, then try some worm portraits, like the one shown here.

The Humble Bee

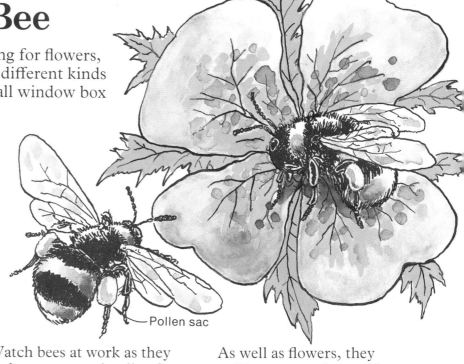

Bees and wasps are always looking for flowers, and if you have a garden several different kinds will probably visit it. Even a small window box with flowers will attract them.

What they are really looking for is their food – nectar – a sweet, sticky liquid made by flowers. As they fly around, pollen grains from the flowers collect on their legs. If they carry this pollen to another flower of the same type they pollinate it and it can then make seeds.

Bumble bees are among the most efficient pollinators in the world. They start work earlier in the morning and finish later in the evening than hive bees, and they don't mind wet weather.

Pollen sac

Watch bees at work as they gather nectar and pollen from flowers. Can you see the pollen sacs on their hind legs? What flowers to they visit?

As well as flowers, they pollinate crop plants. If you have eaten any fruit today, the chances are that a bee helped with the pollination.

Flowers to Attract Bees

Try growing flowers that produce a lot of nectar. Lavender is one of these, and if you know someone with a plant they may give you a cutting. Use scissors to cut through the base of a small branch (late summer is the best time), then plant it in a pot of good soil. Keep the soil damp until the branch grows longer, then plant it in a sunny place. You can also grow flowers for bees from seed. As well as the ones given on page 5, you can try sweet peas and mignonette. The plants shown below are also full of nectar.

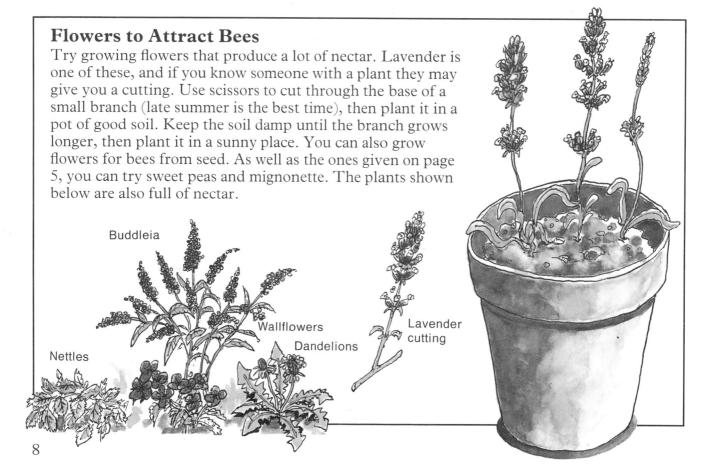

Buddleia

Nettles

Wallflowers

Dandelions

Lavender cutting

The story of a bee colony

1. A single female who has slept through the winter starts a new colony in spring. First, she must find a nesting place.

2. When she has chosen, the female, or queen, collects moss and dry leaves and starts to make a nest.

3. She builds a cup-shaped wax cell, fills it with pollen and honey and lays 12 or more eggs on top.

4. In less than a week, her eggs hatch into grub-like larvae. Their food is soon gone and the queen must find more.

5. After a month, the larvae have turned into young female bees, called workers, but they cannot lay eggs.

6. The queen lays more eggs. The workers care for the larvae and feed them with the food they collect.

7. As the flowers die in the autumn, the hard-working bumble bees die too.

8. A few young queens are reared, and some males to fertilize them.

9. Once fertilized, the queens sleep until spring, when they will start new colonies.

Millions of Ants

Ants are very common insects, and can be found in most gardens where the soil is fairly dry and sandy or gravelly. The types you are most likely to see are the black garden ant, and the red or orange ants.

Try looking under a stone or paving slab in springtime. If you see ants scurrying around and disappearing into holes in the ground, then you have found an ants' nest.

Ants at Home

Most ants live in busy underground colonies, like the one shown above. They use different passages and chambers for storing food, for raising young, or as cemeteries for dead ants.

The colony is ruled by a queen, who lays eggs. Most ants are females, called workers, but like worker bees they do not lay eggs. Some colonies have large workers called soldiers to protect the nest. Male ants have wings, and are seen in summer when they mate with the queens.

Try looking at an ant through a magnifying glass. You will see that it has a very thin waist, six legs, large eyes, and L-shaped antennae, which it uses to feel things and to 'talk' to other ants.

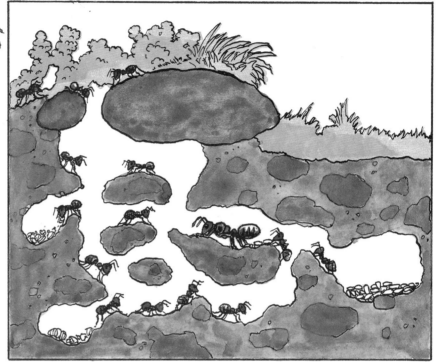

Males – to fertilize the eggs

Queen – to lay eggs

Soldiers – to guard the nest

Workers – to build nest, hunt for food, and care for eggs

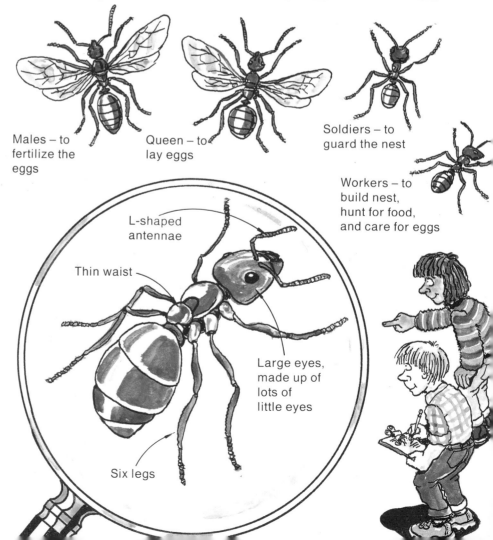

L-shaped antennae

Thin waist

Large eyes, made up of lots of little eyes

Six legs

10

Ants are Amazing

Ants can be pests, but in the garden they do a lot of good work. They get rid of some garden pests, clear away waste, and improve the soil with their digging, making it finer and better for growing plants.

Watching ants at work can be exhausting, because they never seem to stop. If you stay close to a nest and watch as they hurry to and fro you will be astonished at the amount of food they carry.

They often run along in single file carrying bits of wood, dead insects, seeds, pine needles, or bits of scrap food left by humans.

Ants leave a trail of scent as they travel to and from the nest, so other ants can follow. Try blocking their path with a leaf or pebble. See how quickly they move it – or make a new route around it back to the nest.

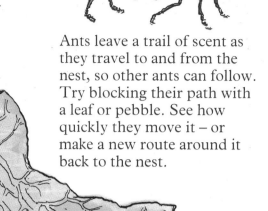

An Ant Maze

If you were an ant, could you find your way from the entrance of the nest to the queen? See how long it takes you.

Weightlifters

Ants are very strong and a single load may weigh 50 times more than the ant. That would be the same as you lifting 50 of your friends!

11

Worthy Weeds

Dandelions, nettles, thistles, brambles and many more plants are known as weeds, and pulled out of the garden as soon as they appear. But these so-called weeds can be useful in attracting wildlife, and pretty to look at too. For example, dandelions attract bees which are good for other plants, nettles provide homes and food for butterflies and other insects, while thistle seeds and brambles provide food for some types of birds.

The Dandelion

Getting rid of a dandelion can be difficult, because it has a long tap root reaching into the ground. If you try and pull it up, the chances are the root will snap off and the dandelion will grow up again.

Apart from producing bright yellow flowers, they have some practical uses. The roots can be made into a drink like coffee. The flowers are sometimes made into wine, or marmalade. The young leaves can be eaten in salad, or fed to your hamster.

Once it has been pollinated the plant makes seeds. The fluffy seed head can contain 200 seeds or more, each with a 'parachute' to help it float away on the breeze. With so many seeds, some are bound to find places to germinate and grow into new plants.

The old game of telling the time with a dandelion 'clock' – blowing on the seed head and counting the number of puffs – is a way of giving nature a hand, but it may not make you very popular with gardeners!

Blackberry Bramble

There are many uses for brambles, apart from making prickly hedges around fields.

The roots can be cooked and eaten as a vegetable, or roasted to make a kind of coffee. The fruit is delicious, and is used for jam, wine or juice, while the stem was used to make rope. It was thought the leaves could heal burns and swellings. After Michaelmas Day, September 29th, it was said to be bad luck to pick blackberries as they were then the Devil's.

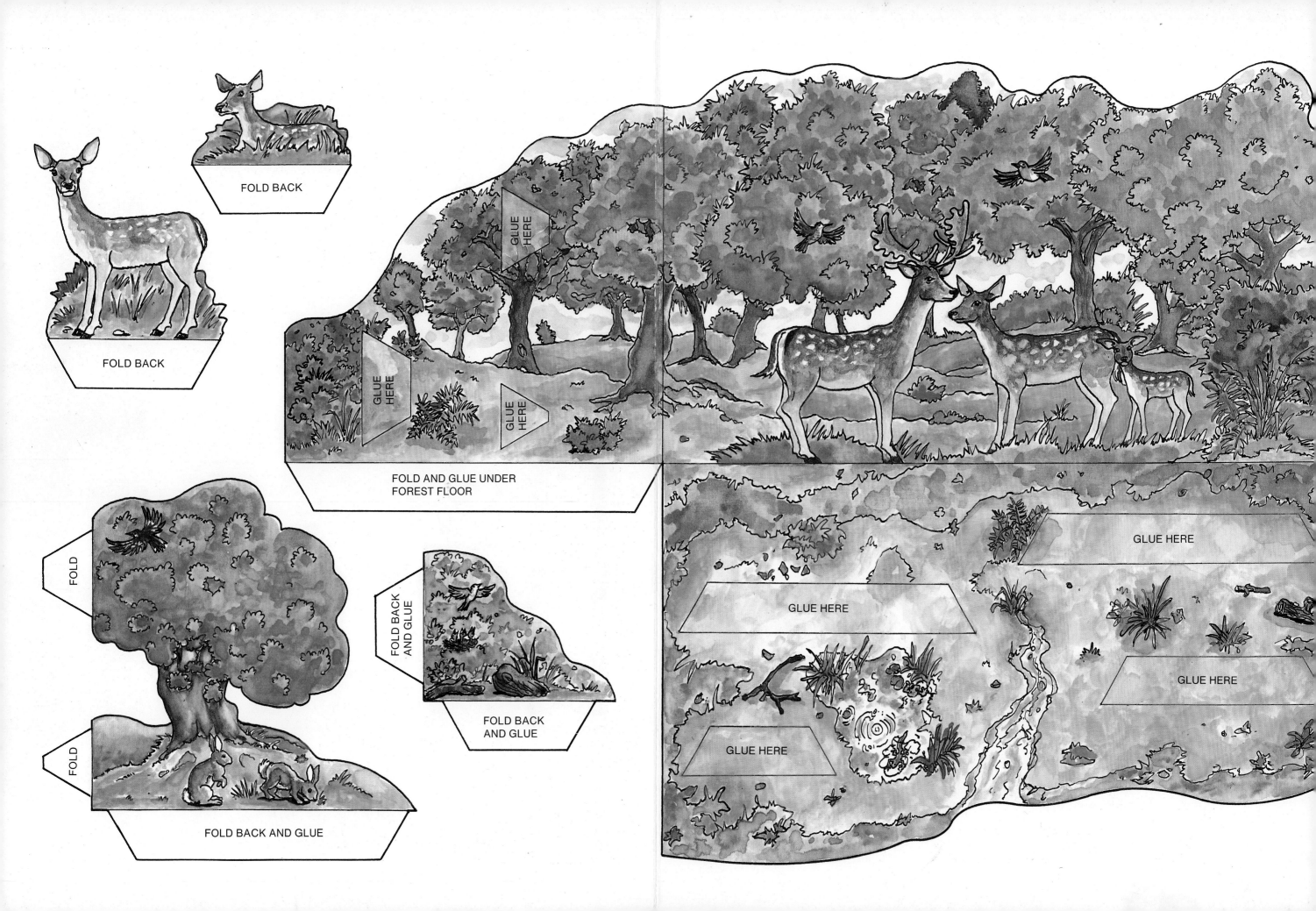

FOLD BACK

FOLD BACK

GLUE HERE

GLUE HERE

GLUE HERE

FOLD AND GLUE UNDER
FOREST FLOOR

FOLD

FOLD

FOLD BACK
AND GLUE

FOLD BACK
AND GLUE

FOLD BACK AND GLUE

GLUE HERE

GLUE HERE

GLUE HERE

GLUE HERE

shown. Glue in the ones at the back of the scene first.

Now you are ready to cut out the animals. Since the shapes are quite complicated, you might find it easier to cut them out roughly first and then more carefully with small scissors.

Bend the flaps back so that the animals stand up firmly. Arrange them in your woodland scene, but don't glue them as you may want to move them around again.

GLUE HERE

GLUE HERE

FOLD AND GLUE UNDER FOREST FLOOR

FOLD BACK

FOLD BACK

FOLD BACK AND GLUE

FOLD BACK AND GLUE

FOLD BACK

FOLD BACK

FOLD BACK

FOLD BACK

FOLD BACK AND GLUE

FOLD BACK

Glue the flaps
in position as
shown

Instructions

Ask an adult to open out the staples in the centre pages of the book. Lift out the card section, then press the staples down again.

Cut out the background for your woodland scene. Fold along the lines as shown to form a box shape. Fold the side flaps and glue them into

position under the base.

Cut out the trees and bushes. Bend the flaps back and glue them to the walls and floor of the scene as

Weed Patch

Try and persuade the gardener in your family to leave a patch for weeds. Dig it over, then leave it completely alone. Watch for a few weeks and make notes on what starts to grow, and when. Keep watching to see which plants are strongest, and which are stifled. The most successful weeds will take over in most situations. Which ones do you think they are?

After a muddy walk, scrape the soil off your boots into a box or tub. Keep the soil damp, and see what starts to grow. You'll be amazed at what you'll find.

Thistles

If you leave a few thistles in your garden, or find a patch of ground where they grow freely, keep an eye on the insects and birds that visit them. Like dandelions, thistles have light seeds with feathery-looking parachutes.

Did you know that if you take the prickles off, and boil the thistle stems they taste rather like rhubarb? It used to be thought that the tallest thistle in the clump belonged to the Devil, and the stems were wizards' walking sticks.

Nettles

Nettles can be very useful in gardens, because they make excellent compost. They store nitrogen in their leaves and, once they have rotted on a compost heap, the nitrogen can be used to help other plants grow healthy leaves. They also provide food for the larvae of butterflies.

Young nettle leaves lose their sting when cooked and make a tasty vegetable, a beer, or tea. They can be used in poultices for bad backs, or in a hair tonic.

Nettle Hair Tonic

You need: a screw top bottle, 500ml of water, a handful of nettles

Boil the nettles in the water for 5 minutes. Use a sieve to drain the liquid into a jug. Pour into the bottle. Apply tonic to your hair after shampooing. Leave for a few minutes then rinse off.

Magic!

Did you know there is magic in your garden? Many of the plants that grow quite commonly have some pretty uncommon beliefs and traditions associated with them. Others can cure illnesses, make perfumes or flavour food.

Here are some old stories about plants. Do you believe them? If you have a honeysuckle or sweetbriar growing over your door it will protect you from witches and fevers.

A juniper bush growing by your house keeps witches at bay – they have to count every leaf before starting any mischief.

Ivy protects against evil. If you wear ivy leaves in your hair, you won't go bald.

Parsley is a magical herb, but it only grows properly if planted by the head of the family. If you plant it on Good Friday, when the Devil is powerless, it grows more quickly. Otherwise it has to visit Satan nine times before getting started.

If you have an apple tree in your garden be sure and leave some small apples on it for the fairies. Then you will have a good crop next year.

Good Companions

Plants have strong likes and dislikes. If planted next to their friends they grow well, but the wrong kind of neighbours can cause great problems.

Strawberries like beans and thyme, but grow badly when near cabbage. Garlic helps roses, potatoes and tomatoes by keeping greenfly and other pests away – they don't like the smell – but it is bad for peas and beans. Wallflowers near to apple trees attract more bees, to help pollination.

Ancient Names

The old names of plants often describe how they grow, or were used in the past.

Another name for scarlet pimpernel is poor man's weatherglass, which closes its petals before rain. Self-heal is a flower that was once used in medicines. It is also called carpenter's herb, perhaps because it was useful when the carpenter cut himself. The word daisy comes from the old name, day's eye, because the flower closes its petals at night.

Herbs and Spices

Can you imagine what meat kept all through winter, without a fridge, would taste like? And what about the smell in a 13th-century castle, where there were no proper toilets, no big windows, fires lit in the middle of the floor and where washing was very uncommon? No wonder our ancestors used herbs and spices to cover up these awful tastes and smells. Herbs were also used in medicines, and sometimes worked very well. This is because some plants contain powerful chemicals, some of which can combat illnesses, while others are poisonous.

An Ointment for Cuts and Grazes

You need: 100g of lard, a good handful of fresh elder-flowers, groundsel and wormwood, and a clean pot with a lid.

Chop the herbs. Ask an adult to help you slowly melt the lard in a saucepan. Add the herbs and simmer for half an hour, stirring often. Strain the melted lard into the pot.

Cover with greaseproof paper and put the lid on. Keep it in the fridge. Use it next time you fall off your bike.

Using Dried Herbs

Pick herbs before they flower, in dry weather. Lay them between old news-paper and place in an airing cupboard. In four days they should be ready to store in jars. Dried herbs keep well for about a year.

Make a herb-flavoured vinegar. To 250ml of red wine vinegar add four basil leaves, or sprigs of thyme.

To 250ml of white wine vinegar add four sprigs of tarragon. Wait a month before using them.

Make scented sachets by filling little cloth bags with cloves, dried orange peel or dried lavender.

To make lavender water, crush a handful of lavender flowers in a bowl and cover with 250ml of boiling water. Leave overnight.

Strain into a bottle with a lid and keep in the fridge.

Lavender water

Herb sachets

Who Lives Here?

If you keep a look out next time you go for a walk, you may find some clues left by the birds and animals that live nearby that will help you guess what they are, or what they were doing. Some of the clues you might find are: feathers – dropped or caught in a bush, or scattered after a kill; footprints in mud or snow; a hole in the ground; or toothmarks on nuts or fruit.

Look Out For:

The silvery trail of a snail or slug early in the morning. Or broken snail shells around a stone, used by a thrush to crack them open.

Gnawed acorns or hazelnuts around the base of a tree, eaten by squirrels.

Bark stripped from a tree, probably by a squirrel.

A pile of snail shells in the grass – if they are crunched up, the snails were eaten by a hedgehog, if a neat hole was made, the culprit was a vole.

Fur caught on fences or bushes, left by an animal on the prowl. These are just some of the clues you might find. Collect or make drawings of any clues you come across, and try to find out who left them.

Animal Search

Can you find these names hidden in the square?

Hedgehog Rabbit   Squirrel
Frog   Mouse   Fox
Snail   Sparrow Earwig
Spider   Badger   Robin

Answers on page 24.

Nibbled hazelnut

```
D J O F E B L E D S N A I L J N F M E O B C Q N C K A
O J G H Q D D K A E J Q O F Q P B K K Q M I I D B J K
K F M F B A F E A P Q I M K K E K F F G K N G O O I B
L I B H N H B D D P B G O J K K K L O D F B N L H Q M
P A S P A R R O W F F H P O D J A O X O H A E I Q A D
A K O F K H N Q J G J I L J N G P D B H P I E P A Q B
O D P O C K M Q K O A N C C F D S L K K E H P D M N D
G L C K C N B D A N N I B B D D P L K B O N K K Q B H
N F I Q H O A J F F J H N O N A I E A F J F N Q M E I
N Q H H C O D N J K G N L D L K D D H D O O L A M M P
M E M O A P G H H G M E H K L N E B E A E E J N P M A
A Q M N E A E J A C Q N M L I E R F B B E K Q H B H P
E F K I L I R Q N J O X N B J K M P L J F P P H N F K
M M P I O N K N L Q P O G G P E M O U S E C P E M O J
M E J P G P A F C H O E F C I K C E K D J E L D M L M
M D D C F G E K A R O D M C Q M Q A K E M P K G A D Q
B B Q F I A C K G O E C E A R W I G N O G A O E A A L
N H B R A B B I T B J Q J L L C N M B I C P D H I D O
F A H Q K O L N F I Q F I Q D J I J L F R O G O C Q N
Q O E O K O K P M N I E S Q U I R R E L M O M G Q N J
J C H D E E J L A D H L M L M C L J M O E Q P C F L A
D M L B E L E H Q Q O J J A H D P C H A B K G I N B J
```

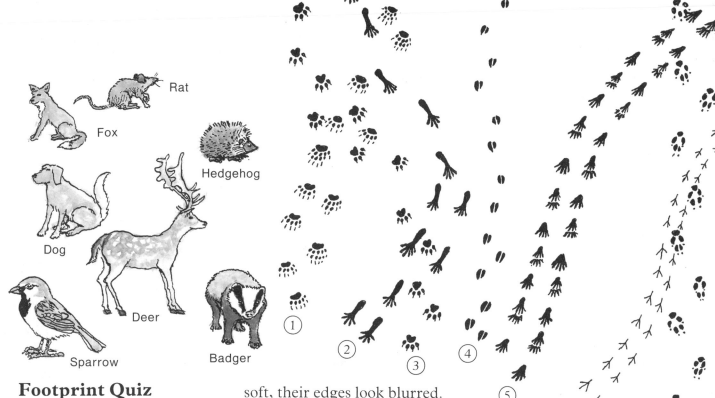

Footprint Quiz

It's fun looking for footprints outside, but it can be hard work. If the ground is too hard the prints don't show up very well, if the ground is too soft, their edges look blurred. Try out your skills on the footprints in this quiz. There are seven trails and seven animals, can you match them up? Answers on page 24.

Food Pellets

You may be lucky enough to have an owl living in your garden, or visiting it at night. If you hear it hooting during the night, look around the base of any large trees in the morning and you might find the owl's food pellets.

Owl pellets are fascinating things to look at. Since owls eat their prey whole – fur, bones, feathers, beaks and all – the pellets contain all the things the owl cannot digest. It just spits them out.

If you find one, place it on a large piece of white paper and carefully pull it apart. You'll be amazed at what you find! See if you can guess the menu of the owl's last meal. It could have been mice or voles, small birds or insects.

Pellets

Brown owl

Look for: Little bones scraps of fur or feather, insect shells

Bits of feather
Jaw bone
Skull
Ribs
Leg bones
Fur

17

Garden Visitors

Some of the birds and animals that visit gardens are so shy you may never actually see them – only the clues they leave. Others are bolder, and can even become regular visitors if you encourage them by leaving food, or growing the right plants to attract them.

The Butterfly Bush

Apart from the plants already mentioned for attracting butterflies, there are various shrubs on which they feed and lay their eggs. Buddleia, or butterfly bush, is one of these. The only problem is the holes the caterpillars eat in the leaves. But once your garden is full of butterflies, you won't mind at all.

Frogs and Fish

If you are lucky enough to have a garden pond, you may find some frogs living by it. A pond with fish and frogs may attract a heron, but although this would be interesting for you, it is bad luck for them as they may end up being eaten!

Hedgehogs

Hedgehogs need to get fatter in autumn to survive the cold winter months. If you see one in your garden you can help by leaving a saucer of dog or cat food out at night, close to where you saw it. Don't leave milk as it is now known to be bad for them. They often hibernate in piles of logs or dry leaves, so search through any bonfires before lighting them. You could save a hedgehog's life.

Food for Birds

It is best to leave food and water out for the birds between October and April – at other times they can find their own. Once you start feeding birds in winter it is vital to keep it up – they come to rely on you.

Many birds love seed cake, made from melted suet with scraps, nuts and seeds mixed into it. But please do not leave salted nuts or dried coconut for them.

Birds also eat seeds and berries from garden plants such as sunflowers, pansies, forget-me-nots and teasels.

As well as eating in your garden, birds will sometimes nest in trees or shrubs, or in nesting boxes you can attach to trees.

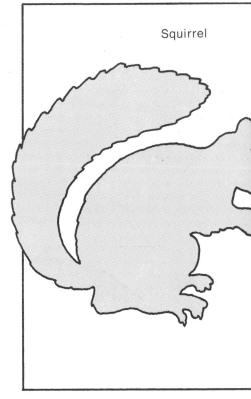

Squirrel

Wall Chart

Trace and cut out the animal shapes below, and any others you can think of. Ask for a long strip of old wallpaper, and stick it to your bedroom wall (pattern side down). Fix the animals along the top and write what you know about each one underneath.

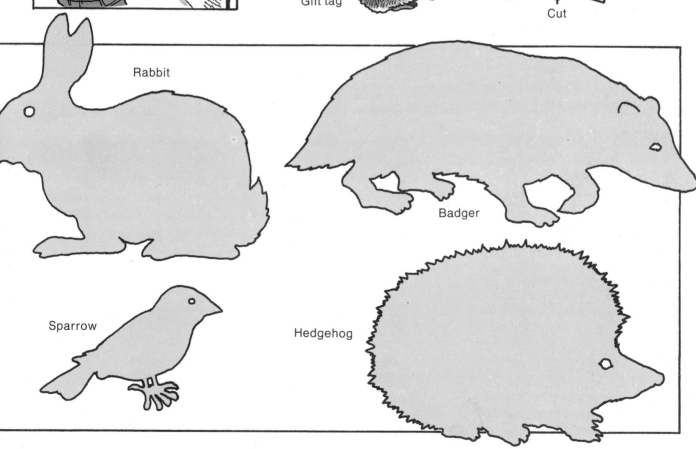

Animal Shapes

Here are some other ideas for things to make:

Trace a shape onto thin card, cut it out and tape a safety pin on the back to make a badge.

Fold some thick paper in half. Trace an animal onto one half so that its back, head or tail is against the fold. Cut through both thicknesses of paper, but leave the fold intact to make a card.

Make gift tags by tracing the shapes onto thin card. Make a hole in the top for a ribbon to tie it on with.

Place-names or game counters can be made by adding a flap onto the bottom of the shape. Cut up the middle of the flap and bend so the animal stands up.

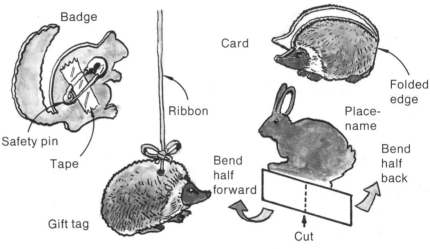

Badge

Safety pin

Tape

Ribbon

Gift tag

Card

Folded edge

Place-name

Bend half forward

Bend half back

Cut

Rabbit

Sparrow

Badger

Hedgehog

High and Mighty

Look up at a tall tree. How old do you think it is? Is it 20, 30, or 100 years old? If it is a large oak or yew tree it could be as many as 500 years old! Just think of all the animals, birds and insects that have relied on it for food and shelter through the years. People have also relied on trees, for firewood and wood for building, and to supply food. It is no wonder that trees have always been thought important and figure largely in our folklore.

The elder has strange beliefs associated with it. It was said to be protected by the 'elder mother', and could not be cut down without asking her. It was also thought to be linked with a goddess of fertility, so the wood was often used to make perches for hen houses so that the hens would lay more eggs.

On a more down to earth level, the stems have been used as pea shooters and whistles for generations.

In parts of Switzerland in the 19th century, a pear tree would be planted for the birth of a girl, and an apple tree for a boy. It was thought that the child would flourish or wither with the tree.

Maple leaves were once used in the storing of apples and root vegetables through the winter. The leaves were thought to keep them fresh.

If an oak tree bears many acorns it is said to mean the next winter will be very cold.

Make a Pink Dye

Look for a piece of bark from a silver birch tree. Scrape off the inside of the bark, and leave it to soak overnight in a saucepan of water. Then simmer it until you get a brownish-red liquid. Drain off the liquid.

You can use this dye on fabric or yarn to give a pink shade. Try boiling a piece of white cotton fabric in the dye for 5 minutes, but test it on a scrap first as the strength of colour is difficult to predict.

Champion Conkers

If you have a horse chestnut tree growing near you, keep a look out in autumn for when the prickly fruits start to fall. Inside them you will find shiny seeds. Collect some and use them to play conkers.

You can make your conkers harder by soaking them over-night in vinegar or salt and water, or by baking them in the oven for half an hour. Or keep some in the dark for a year. Of course, this could be cheating!

Burning Rhyme

This traditional rhyme describes how different types of wood burn.

Beechwood fire burns bright and
  clear,
Hornbeam blazes too.
Keep the logs above a year,
They'll be seasoned through.
Pine is good, so is yew,
For warmth thro' wintry days.
The poplar and the willow too
Take long to make a blaze.
Oaken logs will warm you well
If they are good and dry.
Larch will of the pinewoods smell
And the sparks will fly.
Birchen logs will burn so fast,
Alder not at all.
Chestnut logs for long will last
If cut and let to fall.
Logs of pear and apple logs
Bring scent into the room.
Cherry logs laid on the dogs
Smell like flowers in bloom.
But ashen logs, so smooth and grey,
You burn them green and old.
Cut them, all you can, each day,
They're worth their weight in gold.

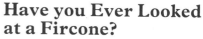

Have you Ever Looked at a Fircone?

Many evergreen trees are cone bearers. Each type has a differently shaped cone, but they are all the same design, look carefully at one. It's nature's way of water-proofing. Can you see the alternate overlapping scales, each one protecting the seed at the base of the one beneath? You will see this same pattern in fish scales, birds' feathers and flower buds. Can you find other examples?

Tree Shapes

Can you identify trees, even at a distance, by their overall shape? Practise with these shapes next time you go out for a walk.

Oak

Plane

Horse chestnut

Elder

Sycamore

Yew

Silver birch

Scots pine

Finders Keepers

You may have found a whole variety of interesting things while you've been out looking at nature. You may even want to start your own collection, but it's helpful to know which things you can keep, and which you should leave.

Things to Collect

Feathers – try and find out which birds they came from.

Snail shells (empty of course) – there are over 25 different types in Britain.

Leaves – but only if you can see plenty of similar ones nearby. It's best not to pick wild flowers, because it is hard to tell which are rare.

Stones, pebbles and empty shells from beaches or river estuaries.

Cones and nuts – try to find different types, or ones that have been nibbled.

Empty shells of birds' eggs, but never take eggs from nests.

Blotting paper

Leaf Press

You can press leaves you find between two pieces of blotting paper, or old newspaper, weighted down with heavy books to keep them flat. After a week or two they should be properly dry.

A Feather Pen

Quill pens, made from feathers, were once used for writing. To make one yourself you need: a strong feather, scissors, paper and ink.

Use scissors to cut the end of the quill at an angle, then cut across the point to make a flat tip. Now cut a slit in the tip so that the knib can spread a little as you press on it. Dip the nib in some ink and you're ready to write. Try cutting different shapes to see which works best.

Cut

Cut

Cut

A Quill pen

A Nature Scrapbook

Make a scrapbook of the things you find. You could organize it by subject, with sections on birds, trees and flowers, or as a diary.

Stick the things you find in your scrapbook along with notes, drawings and photographs. For example, a collection of feathers can be stuck in with photos of birds feeding in your garden, and notes on the food they ate.

To go with pressed leaves, you can take bark rubbings by holding a piece of white paper against the trunk of a tree and rubbing with a wax crayon, and add a photo of the whole tree.

You can press any flowers you grow yourself, or stick the seed packet picture in, with notes on how you grew them. Include poems, stories, recipes or anything you find to make your book special.

Making a Display

Use larger finds to make a display. You can varnish pebbles, rocks and shells to bring out their colours, and label them to show where they came from. Try gluing seeds and nuts onto stiff card to make attractive patterns. More fragile things, like empty birds' eggs or snail shells could be placed on a layer of cotton wool in a box.

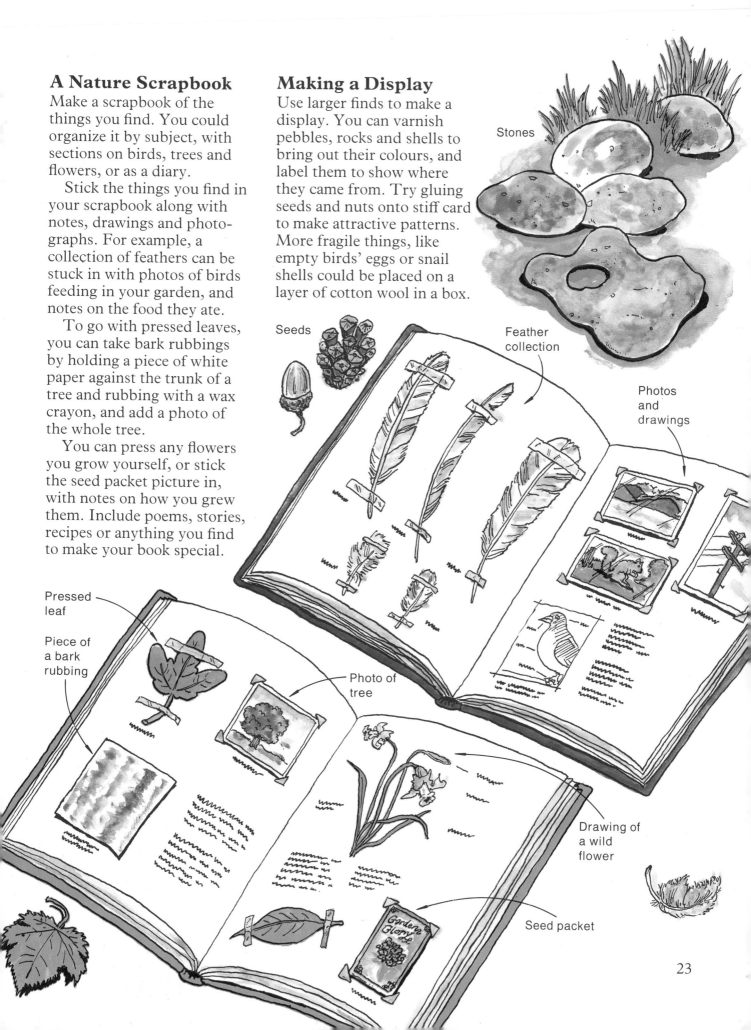

Stones

Seeds

Feather collection

Photos and drawings

Pressed leaf

Piece of a bark rubbing

Photo of tree

Drawing of a wild flower

Seed packet

23

Animal Facts

A bee must visit over 4000 flowers to make a single tablespoon of honey.

There are 5.3 million cats in Britain – one for every ten people.

The red squirrel is one of the most popular animals – with fleas that is. Over 13,000 fleas were once found on a single squirrel.

At night, the eyesight of a barn owl is one hundred times sharper than that of a human.

Roe deer can run at speeds of up to 64km/h for short periods.

The smallest wild mammal in Britain is the pygmy shrew – its head and body are only 45–60mm long.

Answers

Page 17: Footprint Quiz

1 Badger
2 Rat
3 Dog
4 Deer
5 Hedgehog
6 Sparrow
7 Fox

Page 16: Animal Search

```
D J O F E B L E D S N A I L J N F M E O B C Q N C K A
O J G H Q D D K A J Q O F Q P B K K Q M I I D B J K
K F M F B A F E A P Q I M K K E K F F G K N G O O I B
L I B H N H B D D P B G O J K K K L O D F B N L H Q M
P A S P A R R O W F F H P O D J A O X O H A E I Q A D
A K O F K H N Q J G J I L J N G P D B H P I E P A Q B
O D P O C K M Q K O A N C C F D S L K K E H P D M N B
G L C K C N B D A N N I B B D D P L K B O N K K Q B H
N F I Q H O A J F F J H N O N A I E A F J F N Q M E I
N Q H H C O D N J K G N L D L K D D H D O O L A M M P
M E M O A P G H H G M E H K N E B E A E E J N P M A
A Q M N E A E J A C Q N M L I E R F B B E K Q H B H P
E F K I L I R Q N J O X N B J K M P L J F P P H N F K
M M P I O N K N L Q P O G G P E M O U S E C P E M O J
M E J P G P A F C H O E F C I K C E K D J E L D M L M
M D D C F G E K A R O D M C Q M Q A K E M P K G A D Q
B B Q F I A C K G O E C E A R W I G N O G A O E A A L
N H B R A B B I T B J Q J L L C N M B I C P D H I D O
F A H Q K O L N F I Q F I Q D J I J L F R O G O C Q N
Q O E O K O K P M N I E S Q U I R R E L M O M G Q N J
J C H D E E J L A D H L M L M C L J M O E Q P C F L A
D M L B E L E H Q Q O J J A H D P C H A B K G I N B J
```

KINGFISHER
An imprint of Larousse plc
Elsley House, 24-30 Great Titchfield Street,
London W1P 7AD
First published in 1988 by Kingfisher

10 9 8

Text Copyright © Manor Lodge Productions Ltd 1988
Illustrations Copyright © Grisewood & Dempsey Ltd 1988

BRITISH LIBRARY CATALOGUING IN PUBLICATION DATA
Osband, Gillian
    Nature.
    1. Gardens – For children
    I. Title   II. Simonds, David   III. Series
    712'.6
ISBN 0 86272 367 1

Edited by Jacqui Bailey and Meg Sanders
Designed by Ben White
Cover design by David Jefferis
Phototypeset by Southern Positives and Negatives (SPAN), Lingfield, Surrey
Printed in Spain